Your Best
Life = Action!

Your Best Life = Action!

3 Steps to Accelerate Your Financial Progress, Kill Debt, and Enjoy Everyday Life

Ivory Hodges

www.debtfreebie.com

ISBN-13: **9780692729779**
ISBN-10: **0692729771**

Contents

Introduction

Inside every fascinating book emerges powerful information that transforms lives. Where are you now with managing your finances? Are you tired of living paycheck to paycheck? Do you find yourself unable to save money no matter how hard you try? Do you want to kick all your debts to the curb in a fraction of the time? Whether you are in good financial shape or in need of some financial fitness, 'Your Best Life=Action!' will give you the motivation to take control of your financial future and achieve peace of mind. This book is an easy-to-read guide that will help you stay focused on your goals.

This book is not about theory or about the technical aspects of personal finance. Each chapter gives short, straight to the point information, author's tips, and powerful insights to help you live your best life now. You will learn how to take action now and stop procrastination dead in its tracks! With intensity, focus, discipline, and sacrifice, you will experience total freedom in a fraction of the time. You'll gain a sense of direction. Your family and relationships will flourish. You'll leave a solid legacy for your children and you'll be able to give like never before. So, turn the page and let's get started!

Part 1:
Consider Change, Not Your
Circumstances

Creating a New Relationship with Money

I grew up in a family of three boys and three girls. I was the middle child, so I got away with a lot more than my two older brothers did. (I was the baby boy, and my parents spoiled me.) One of my older brothers and I didn't have the best relationship when we were kids. I always found a way to annoy him. I looked up to my older brothers, but I wasn't cool enough to hang around them. I thought I was the coolest little brother on the planet! How in the world could they not want to hang out with me? As we got older, we started to bond through watching wrestling together. We were huge World Wrestling Entertainment (WWE) fans.

We would imitate our favorite characters and even wear their wrestling gear. One day we were all at home watching one of the pay-per-view wrestling events. My elder brother was a major fan of Dwayne "The Rock" Johnson, and I liked Paul Michael "Triple H" Levesque. They were set to fight in the main event match at WrestleMania 2000. We both cheered our favorites on as they made their entrance into the ring. Before the match started, I made a bet with one of my brothers to heighten the suspense. If Triple H won the match, my brother would have to buy me lunch, and if The Rock won, I would agree to wear The Rock's T-shirt for a whole day.

We shook hands and made the deal. We were both on the edge of our seats as the two heavy-weights went at each other. Up until the wrestling match, my brother and I had never spent that much time together, let alone agreed on something. Suddenly, a shift took place. We talked about sports, girls, and movies, among other things. I thought to myself, *He's not so bad after all*. The fight was coming down to the end, and eventually my favorite wrestler won the match. I had won the bet! After the event was over, we talked about the highlights of the fight. We had so much fun together. That night was a turning point in our relationship. Eventually, we became close brothers and ultimately best friends. To this day, we have a great relationship and understanding of each other. Things began to change as we set our differences aside and realized that we had more in common with each other than we had thought.

Similar to the relationship I initially had with my brother, many people have a strained relationship with money. At one point in time, they had dreams of financial security and independence, but sadly, they've given up on those dreams. I'm sure you've heard people say things like "I just want to be comfortable." They seek this comfort by spending money on things that make them feel good in the moment; however, these temporal things end up costing them in the long run. Unfortunately, they seek comfort today because they don't believe they will have the future they once hoped for.

Maybe you've heard people say things like "I'm not good with money" or "I can't save money because I have a spending problem" or "Money can't buy you happiness."

I remember talking to a young lady about the importance of saving money for the future, and she was quick to say, "You can't take it with you, so spend it like it's your last. YOLO." You only live once, right? This mind-set is so ingrained in our culture that it will take a total transformation to change it.

When I was young I made really dumb decisions with money. I viewed money as if it was just paper and coins, a means to get whatever I saw on TV and other things I wanted. I also had a strained relationship with money. I bought into the same mentality many people have about money. Since money didn't come very often, I spent it faster than you could say, "Rubber baby buggy bumpers!" I didn't respect money. It was this lack of respect that caused me to have a distorted view of money. Doctor Phil once said that if you don't have a healthy level of respect for something, the tendency is to treat it as disposable. I grew up in a poor family with limited resources. I felt like we were always going to be poor and that money, wealth, and opportunities were reserved only for special people. Call me crazy, but I had a love-hate relationship with money.

During the financial crisis of 2008, I was completely clueless about what was going on. Every news station was saying the same thing—predicting that we were headed for financial Armageddon and that the economic "Titanic" was sinking. I was very nervous because I didn't know much about money. I was consumed with the news, trying to find out what was going to happen next. Large companies that had been around for decades—and in some cases more than a century—were collapsing left and right. Every day offered a new story. One day I decided to take my head out of the sand, try to understand what was going on, and learn how money truly worked. I started reading blogs, purchasing subscriptions to financial magazines, going to personal-finance conferences, and getting my hands on anything and everything that had to do with money management. I became obsessed with the process of learning about money, so much so that I found myself reading and studying more frequently than I was spending time with friends and family members.

The deeper I got into the world of money, the more I began to reflect on my childhood. Poverty now began to make sense to me. We dwelled in a vicious cycle by living day to day instead of looking beyond the moment. Investing in the future hadn't even been on the radar. Like most Americans, our family lived paycheck to paycheck with no savings set aside, so even when the slightest emergency happened, it put us in a financial hole. Don't get me wrong; my parents did the best they could to provide us with a decent upbringing, and they were doing all they knew how to do.

I would go on to spend the next three years learning about how to make money, spend it wisely, and grow it through investing. I accumulated a wealth of knowledge through self-education. I was thrilled at what I was learning. I would talk about money with anyone who was willing to listen to me.

With this newfound knowledge, I wanted to help people in my community through financial literacy. I started holding small group meetings at my house to share what I'd learned. I taught fundamental money-management principles such as the value of money, savings, debt, and so on.

People were hungry for the information. Like me years earlier, many didn't know the basic principles of personal finance, and they were grateful for the meetings. As time went on, I started to notice how some of the group members were a bit apprehensive. It was as if they didn't have the confidence to manage their own finances. They were learning a great deal about money management, but there seemed to be deeply ingrained ideologies about money that caused hesitation. Learning about money management was a good start, but more needed to be done in order to apply the information. The information was helpful, but old habits, mind-sets, and behaviors die hard. Many people who were coming to the meetings shared how they'd had plenty of negative experiences with their finances.

The lightbulb moment came when I was thinking about ways to translate knowledge and wisdom into action plans and eventually small steps of change. I knew that knowledge was half the problem. We live in the information age; we have more information available to us than at any other time in history. Many of us know that we should be saving more money, spending our hard-earned money more wisely, getting out of debt, and so on, but the problem isn't knowing what to do; it's getting it done!

I started having group discussions about general attitudes about finances. I wasn't surprised by what most people brought up in the meetings. One woman said money ruled her life. She explained how for all her working life she was chasing money, living paycheck to paycheck. She was working harder than her money was working. She went on to explain that she had never been good at saving money and that she had a spending habit that was out of control.

Another member of the group shared how good his parents had been with money. They had a healthy level of respect for their money and managed it very well. However, his parents were hoarders and penny pinchers. They were extremely frugal, to the point that he thought his childhood had been hindered because his parents rarely spent money on fun and entertaining stuff because it "wasn't in the budget." This upbringing made him feel like he didn't want to live as his parents had, so when he started working, he made sure he was not going to be controlled by being a cheapskate.

He purchased whatever he wanted without putting away funds for a rainy day or planning for the future; he was a "right now" person.

Many of the behaviors brought up in the meetings were based on how the participants' upbringings had shaped their views on money. I knew there had to be a way for people to be free of their past relationships and experiences with finances. If only there was a way for people to slowly wean themselves off old ideologies and start embracing a new way moving forward.

One day I was watching Doctor Oz's TV program, and the discussion was about breaking old habits. The guest that was on the show had shared some valuable information on how habits are shaped and tips on how to form new habits. I was glued to the TV, desperately trying to follow every word. This topic was very interesting to me because I was in the process of kicking my junk-food habit. I was the snack king, who would whip up creative snacks in fifty different ways and post them on Facebook and Instagram just for the fun of it. I absolutely loved snacking!

The first step on the road to recovery is admitting you have a problem and that you're powerless over it. I was ashamed to admit that I was the poster child for chips, candy, soda, and whatever sweets I could get my hands on! I also knew this was not good for me considering the numerous health problems running through my family such as diabetes and high blood pressure. Long-term health is something I consider very important, and if I was going to live a long, healthy life, I would have to adjust my diet and, most importantly, change the way I viewed myself. The cares and pressures of life had me trapped in my own little tunnel view. I couldn't see anything beyond my current situation and circumstances. I wasn't thinking about the future; I had all my eggs in today's basket.

I didn't have time (or at least I thought I didn't) for vision casting or dreaming about the possibilities of what life could be. The day-to-day grind was no joke! The struggle was real. I was balancing working at two jobs, going to school, studying, and spending time with family and friends. My life was complicated and busy. I didn't have time to sit down and plan out my meals for the day. I was one of those picker uppers; I would grab food on the go, and that would be my breakfast, lunch, snacks, and dinner.

By the grace of God, I did not have any health issues during my head-in-the-sand moments of constantly pigging out with unhealthy foods. I wanted to get off the junk-food roller coaster, so I tried dieting. Albert Einstein once said that the definition of insanity is doing the same thing over and over again and expecting different results. I was eating junk food for breakfast, lunch, and dinner but was expecting to properly fit in a slim-fit suit—not going to happen. Now it's been a few years since I graduated from high school, and I weigh a little less than 175 pounds.

Now that I had officially became an "adult"—you know, when you have a super-busy life filled with work, meetings, and a to-do list—I no longer had free time to exercise or cook my meals. I needed the secret pill that would help me get back into shape without having to exercise. I wanted to have my ice cream and eat my cake too. But I knew that there was no easy way out; there would be no shortcuts home. I would have to learn how to better manage my workload: school, family, and personal time. I didn't know where to start.

I feel sorry for people who lived before the days of the Internet and GPS. Nowadays, whenever we don't know something or want to learn about anything, what do we do? Google it! So I would read dozens of articles and blogs that provided tons of information about what to eat and what not to eat.

The Internet is information overload! There's so much information available at the click of a mouse. Much of the content I found online conflicted with other content, so I quickly became overwhelmed and, soon after, quit. Next, I tried changing grocery stores. The local chain store I shopped at carried more sweets than a fat kid's snack drawer. It was as if all the unhealthy foods were placed up front because they knew we were too lazy to look for our drug of choice, which is sugar. They made it very convenient for us to grab snacks and bust right through the door only to come back for more. If you wanted healthier options, you would have a difficult time finding them. It was like going to Walmart trying to find basic hygiene products but ending up in the electronics aisle. I felt like a rat going through a maze looking for cheese on a mousetrap.

I eventually started going to a grocery chain store that had a reputation for better-quality foods and was geared toward the health-consciousness movement that was taking place in Detroit at the time. The first time I walked into the store, I noticed that the atmosphere was completely different from those in stores I had previously shopped at. In the front of the store was fresh fruits, vegetables, and other healthy products. The meats were fresh, and even the snacks contained less sugar and other artificial flavors. Even the egg section was impressive. The store had ten different egg brands with fancy health-nut language that only the über-food-conscious gurus knew. The staff at the grocery store was also very helpful. They assisted me in identifying suitable foods to meet my health and fitness goals.

The prices were a bit higher than what I was accustomed to, but it was worth the investment. I spent nearly an hour checking the store out, finding new foods and recipes to accompany my total health makeover. As I was standing in the checkout lane, an announcement was made over the PA system that the store was having a monthly community meeting to offer fitness and well-being tips and healthy recipes. I was super impressed! When I got to the front of the lane and put my groceries on the conveyer belt, I kindly greeted the cashier. She was very polite and said that I must be a newbie. "How did you know that?" I asked. She smiled and said, "You have the newbie sticker on." I forgot that when I had first walked into the store they had asked if I was new to the store and had given me a sticker. I told the cashier that I was trying to change my eating habits.

She mentioned that I have more control over what I eat than what I think. She went on to say that oftentimes we need to change our environment in order to allow new information to usher in change. She was confident that I would notice the difference in taste and that over time my body would thank me for taking small steps toward change. She invited me to a documentary viewing that was taking place at the local library. She said the film highlighted the benefits of a healthy lifestyle change and the dangers of unhealthy eating. I thought to myself, *This is just what I need! I want to be in great shape and have the energy to maintain an active life.* I told her I would be there. As promised, I showed up at the library to watch the documentary. The information was very powerful.

That day, my life completely changed. No longer did I see myself the same way. I started viewing my body as a temple and started to believe that I am what I eat. It didn't happen overnight, but I slowly started changing my lifestyle. I retired from being the king of snacks and became the man with carrots, apples, and vitamins. I started going to the community meetings at the grocery store. I figured that I needed to be around like-minded people who had similar goals to mine. The people who came to the meetings were always encouraging and were generally happy people. I could tell that most of them had an improved quality of life because of the choices they'd made.

This was a special place where I could escape from the rat race—the high-speed, go-go-go life that had my head spinning out of control. It was my outlet from reality, where fast food and convenience stores were on every corner. Within fifty days I lost thirteen pounds and felt great! I had more energy, even after the longest of days. I was more productive, and it seemed as if I had more time in my day to do extra things like cook meals and hang out with friends.

Today, I live a totally different lifestyle than I did a few years ago. I still go out to restaurants once in a blue moon. Every once in a while I'll grab a candy bar, but not nearly as often as I used to. Hearing the constant compliments I receive about my weight loss never grows old! Flexing my muscles in the mirror without having to suck in my gut is the ultimate reward. Occasionally, I like to reflect on where I am and how far I've come. I thought to myself, *How could I have so much power and control over other areas of my life, but at one point in time I couldn't even resist the temptation of a cupcake?* What gave me the motivation to want to change my behavior in order to end my daily love affair with snacks and fast food?

I had my "aha" moment! You know, that moment when the lightbulb finally comes on. I had to change the way I saw myself. It started with having the right perspective about my health and seeing how unhealthy portions of snacks could be detrimental to my future well-being. I eventually started working out, eating better foods, and snacking less. Again, it didn't happen overnight, but I finally started to gain control of my eating habits. When I went to the grocery or convenience store, I no longer felt like I was on autopilot, grabbing snacks without even thinking about it.

It's the same way with managing finances—there must be a change in mind-set. Good money-management behaviors are developed when we have a healthy view of and perspective on our life, family, and finances. Our brains are like supercomputers. We can program them to meditate on whatever we decide. Why not choose to put your thoughts to good use by dwelling on the possibilities? If you think you can't save money, then you won't. If you tell yourself that you'll never get out of debt, then you can't. One of the keys to having financial peace is shifting your relationship to money toward the proper prospective. It doesn't matter how bad you have been with managing your finances up until this point; you can decide to take a leap of faith and choose to do things in a different way. The hardest battle you may face is looking at yourself in the mirror and confessing that you need to do better. Can I tell you something? We all have room for improvement.

Easy credit has allowed many of us to create a false image of status and clout. We can purchase the latest car, get the newest piece of technology, swipe the credit card for high-end clothes, and live in well-kept neighborhoods, all for a monthly payment. We can even go to the local pet store and take home Pixy the friendly dog for ninety days, same as a cash-interest loan. With unlimited options to spend money on, we need a sense of purpose, a cause to commit to in order to point our finances in the right direction. Having that "mirror talk" will allow you to be honest with yourself. The truth can hurt at times, but the truth can also save your life or maybe even your marriage.

When you take the time to reflect on where you've been, where you are, and where you are headed, something weird happens. You start weeding out the things that are not important and start focusing on what really matters to you. When you are mindful of the fact that you have children and want to send them to college someday, you will be more thoughtful about saving for their college funds. "Retirement" won't be a dirty procrastination word when you think about priorities and what kind of lifestyle you want to have during your golden years.

A change in attitude, outlook, and perspective will lead you in the right direction. One of the best things we can do is to be completely honest with ourselves. Once we get real with ourselves, then we can begin to take baby steps toward transformation. It won't happen overnight, but a metamorphosis will start to take place. Also, changing your relationship with money has everything to do with facing your fears. If you dread when bills come due or are reluctant to track spending, then that may be a sign of avoiding bigger issues. Facing the truth about your financial situation may shock you at first.

You may say, "I'm spending one hundred twenty-five dollars a month on coffee? Wow! I only have a few hundred dollars in my savings account!" or "Where does my money go? Most of my money is going to my student loans and car payment? Oh my goodness!" The discovery of the truth about your finances will actually point you in the right direction. There's no greater feeling than having a fresh start. But you have to be willing to stop wandering around and find out where you are, financially speaking.

A few years ago, I went to Mall of America in Bloomington, Minnesota, one of the largest malls in the country.

I was looking for a particular electronics store to purchase a few items I needed. I prefer shopping online because it's much easier for me to get what I'm looking for with the click of a mouse. However, I was in the area, so I decided to go to the mall. Also, the store was having a clearance sale. I had never been to this particular mall before. I walked around the mall for nearly two hours aimlessly, looking for the store. All I had to do was look at the mall map with the red marker that says "You are here." I would have been able to locate where I was and head in the store's direction. I would have saved myself a lot of time and trouble. It would have been much easier to find the store, get what I needed, and be on my way. After looking at the mall directory, I noticed that I had passed the store three times!

Here's my point: you don't have to wander through life hoping things will get better. Locate where you are on your financial road map, and see if you are on the right track. If not, then make some changes. It's good to have faith in and a positive outlook about the future, but more times than not, if you're not actively doing something about your situation, you can expect more of the same results. Life is complicated, but your finances don't have to be. Getting a good understanding of where you are financially should motivate you to take action.

If you do not have a clue about the state of your finances, now is the time to pause, look at the financial map, and see where you are. Most people would rather not know what's going on because they refuse to deal with the truth. The truth can be scary, so it's human nature to procrastinate about making changes. Procrastination is our greatest enemy. But there's no time like the present. Now is the time to do something about your situation. You don't have to wander aimlessly through life not knowing whether you are going to be able to live a comfortable life.

You can no longer turn a blind eye to your financial situation and pretend that everything is fine when your wallet is screaming at you. As hard as this may sound, you have to embrace where you are right now. This will allow you to have a sober view and take baby steps on the right path instead of walking through the wilderness without a clear road. Nobody would prefer not to have money set aside for emergencies or would rather work until they are one hundred years old just to be able to pay bills and have a decent lifestyle. Suddenly, life would have passed by, and, before you know it, there would not be much to show for it. Suddenly, the children are ready to go off to college; before you know it, you will be at retirement age.

My encouragement for you is to be open to receive a different way of living—a change in the way you see yourself, your community, life in general, and your loved ones. As you begin to discover life in a whole new way, you will soon see acceleration. Suddenly things that stressed you out will not even merit your attention. Keeping up with the Joneses won't matter anymore; besides, I've talked with the Joneses, and they let me in on their little secret: they, too, are broke! Needing to have the latest and greatest technology won't be necessary. This journey of creating a new relationship with your finances will enhance your life and give you the financial peace you deserve.

2

Get Ready for Change

I heard about this study that scientists conducted. They had five monkeys and a pole with bananas at the top of the pole. Every time a monkey went up the pole, a scientist would pour cold water on the other monkeys. After this happened several times, whenever a monkey went up the pole to get a banana, the other monkeys would beat him up. After a while, no monkey wanted to go up the pole to get a banana.

The scientists then swapped one of the monkeys for a totally new one. The new monkey went up the pole to grab a banana, and the other monkeys immediately started beating him up. After several attempts, the new monkey learned not to go up the pole to grab the bananas even though he never understood why.

Another monkey was brought in, and the same thing happened. The first swapped monkey joined in on the beating of the second swapped monkey. A third monkey was exchanged with the same result: a beating by the other monkeys. A fourth and fifth monkey was substituted, and the same thing happened, a beating by the other monkeys. The results were that five monkeys who had never had cold water poured on them continued to beat up any monkey who attempted to go up the pole and grab a banana. If the monkeys could talk, I bet one of them would say, "That's just the way things are done around here."

Here's what I want you to understand: we all have unconscious attitudes about money that have a direct correlation to our financial behaviors. Some money habits that we inherited from our parents, society, community, and so on must be questioned. One of the keys to life is constantly embracing change. Most people don't like change. We drive the same route to work, eat the same foods, park in the same spots, and, if we aren't careful, wear the same underwear! At the beginning of a new year, many people have goals to improve their lives. Unfortunately, most don't follow through with their goals. By embracing change, we position ourselves to benefit tremendously in life.

This is what my good friend Tim did. Tim is a gifted drummer. He's been playing the drums since he was four years old. He has aspirations to become a world-class drummer. There are plenty of talented drummers who are capable of playing high-quality music. Although Tim knew that he was gifted when it came to playing the drums, he also knew he couldn't depend on his talent alone. He used to always say that hard work beats talent when talent doesn't work hard. He would continually work hard at improving his skills. Every day Tim would practice his craft.

Occasionally, he entered drum-off competitions to see how he fared against his peers. Win, lose, or draw, Tim would continue to change his game as he learned from other musicians. He knew that in order to be the best drummer that he could be, learning new skills and adapting to change would be essential. One day he decided to enter a drum competition with some of the best drummers in his area. He had to bring his best game if he was going to have a chance. Long story short, he finished in the top rankings in the drum competition. How did he do it? He embraced change and continued to work on his skills.

What am I saying? If you want to get the most out of your hard-earned money, you will have to be open to change and learn new financial-management skills. Technology has made it far easier for us to manage our finances in a whole new way. There are tons of creative apps that allow you to track your spending, reward yourself for saving money, find online coupons, and more! I recommend using Mint app because it allows you to see all your balances and transactions together. The application pulls all your financial information into one place so you can see your entire financial picture, and it also tracks your spending and automatically categorizes it for you. The EveryDollar app is also another good budgeting tool as well. The app makes it easy for you to track transactions and check your budget on the go. There are many more apps that can help you manage your finances and leverage your time. The Internet has made it much more convenient to pay bills online without ever having to mail in a payment or drive around town. You have the option to pay your bills within seconds, saving you time.

Change can be hard, especially if you have been doing something a certain way for a long period of time. I believe that most people are ready for change. They want to be prepared for emergencies. They want to organize their finances and save for the future. But many times they have been programmed to focus on the here and now, financing their present lifestyles with little regard for the future. Shifting your direction toward living life with a purpose will help you understand and commit to what's truly important to you. Having a sense of direction will also keep you on the right course.

Ask yourself these four questions:

- What are the things that and who are the people who truly matter most in my life?
- What do I need to spend more or less time on?
- Why don't I do the things I know I should be doing?
- What could I do today to improve?

Without focus in life, we drift without any real sense of fulfillment. A life without purpose is a life without a destination. A long-distance marathon runner knows that he or she has to be in great shape before the race begins. They need to focus their training efforts in a way that will assist them in achieving their goals.

Consider this: money is amoral. It needs a master to tell it what to do. Your purpose in life should be to be your money's new boss. If you want to retire with dignity, you will want to prioritize savings. Tired of robbing Peter to pay Paul? Intentionally set your mind to organizing your budget, reducing spending, and not borrowing more money. Most of our money habits and principles can be traced back to our behaviors. Many of us know that we should be saving money for the future, getting out of debt, and living within our means. The problem isn't knowing what to do; it's getting the job done! Dave Ramsey says that personal finance is 80 percent behavior and only 20 percent actual knowledge. In other words, in order to win with money you have to pay attention to your habits. Start taking notice of how and when you spend money.

When you're depressed, do you go to the mall for retail therapy? Do you shop impulsively when you're out and about? What are your spending patterns on the weekends or when out with friends and family? Having a clear understanding of why and how you spend your money is one of the first steps toward making changes.

We live in the most marketed culture in the history of mankind. Market-savvy companies persuade us to buy now and pay later. Don't think about your future; right now you can have it all. The idea is that if you buy the products, you will be happier and more successful, look younger, and feel better. In some cases this simply isn't true. On a regular basis, we need to renew our minds from all the corporate brainwashing and marketing schemes. It doesn't matter how much our culture worships money and material things; our self-worth should always outweigh our net worth.

At the end of the day, what matter most are healthy relationships with family and friends, being in good physical health, enjoying your career, and making a difference in the community. I remember watching a movie called *The Joneses*. The movie was

about a seemingly perfect couple and their attrac-
tive teenage children who were the envy of their
neighborhood. The suburban community was filled
with beautiful homes with nice cars and all the
other expensive toys people crave. The wife was
the definitive fashion queen! She was drop-dead
gorgeous; she wore nothing but the latest fashion
clothing, and was decked out in all designer labels.

The husband was charismatic and successful.
He had a prosperous business, a sexy wife, a big
house, and all the latest gizmos and gadgets. The
two teenage children were wildly popular in their
new school. They were intelligent and flaunted
their parents' success. But as the neighbors tried
to keep up with this perfect family, they were completely caught off guard when they found out that
the so-called perfect family really wasn't a family at all. They were hired sales professionals who
were in the business of selling the fantasy dream of
having it all: wealth, prestige, beauty, a big house,
and so on. What appears to be the perfect family
and ideal life isn't necessary a reality.

What's my point? When you compare yourself
to others, you are chasing a dream lifestyle you

may never obtain. You run the risk of living a life of constant dissatisfaction. You will always need more to quench your appetite. It's like running on a treadmill—you're moving but not going anywhere. If anything, you are wearing yourself out! Could it be that the reason we have so many health problems is because we carry so many unnecessary burdens? Have we become so obsessed with attaining the ideal lifestyle that we have lost our sense of self-worth?

I'm asking you to get ready for change. We are not always going to be here. Life is short. Your purpose is too great; your assignment is too valuable. Rise up and live every aspect, including the direction of your finances, with conviction and purpose. Start building up buffers of resistance to impulsive shopping. Get in the habit of asking these questions before every purchase:

- Do I need this?
- Why am I here?
- Where will I put it?
- How will I pay for it?
- How do I feel?

Don't fall for the lie that changing direction is impossible.

Years ago, every year around Thanksgiving time, a couple of my friends and I would go Black Friday shopping. This is a day when most companies offer deep discounts and deals on their products and services to entice you to spend money. I started talking to one of my friends about how I had saved up money to get an electronic item I had wanted for a while. While I was in line at the store, there was a woman who mentioned that she would go broke to get everything she wanted. She said she tried to save money, but her impulses would always win. In a way, I felt as though she was saying you only live once (YOLO), so live in the moment. So many people have the YOLO mentality. They live for today, without giving much thought to the future. I say this respectfully: this is a major reason so many people are broke!

Another important area we need to change is saving money. Sometimes the hardest thing about saving money is that you aren't used to saving money. There are plenty of reasons people don't save money. In my experience as a financial coach,

I've heard some common reasons. The YOLO mentality is probably the number-one reason. Benjamin Franklin said there are only two things in life that are certain: death and taxes. This couldn't be truer! So why save money if you can't take it with you when you die? Well, for one, your final expenses and other personal costs don't stop when you pass away.

If you do not have life insurance or adequate coverage, you could find yourself in an even bigger financial hole, leaving the burden on your loved ones. This can be avoided by having adequate life insurance. We need a little protection in life. We never know when something might happen, so it is good practice to have coverage set aside just in case. Proverbs 13:22 says, "A good person leaves an inheritance for their children's children." The YOLO mentality can make it much harder on those coming after you. You *can* enjoy everyday life *and* manage your personal finances.

Another common reason people don't save money is because they procrastinate. The thought is *I'll eventually get around to it*. This is a huge financial mistake! You are missing out on the power of compounding! There are millions of ways to explain what compounding means, but let's just say that it is a mathematical explosion. In addition, $2 + 2 + 2 = 6$, but with compounding, $2 \times 2 \times 2 = 30$, which means your money is earning interest on top of interest, which allows it to grow much faster. Here's an example: if you were to sock away $50 per month (coffee and vending machine money) for ten years at say, 10 percent, your money would grow to $10,518! That's how compound interest works. Now, if you don't save money, it will be very difficult to grow your money. Zero times a million is still zero. Procrastination will rob you of all the benefits of compound interest working in your favor.

Reason number three that people don't save money is because there is always an excuse or reason for buying something. There's nothing wrong with having the latest and greatest TVs, cars, and technology. Heck, I want the fancy toys too! When I'm shopping for something, I, too, have impulsive thoughts racing through my mind. *The upgraded model makes my current cell phone outdated and lame. The upgraded cell phone whispers, Upgrade if you want to stay relevant.* As soon as I get suckered into buying the new phone, in just a few months, there is a newer piece of technology that is supposed to be the next big thing, which again, makes my new cell phone, which I had just purchased a few months ago, outdated. The cycle never ends!

There will always be a newer car model, an upgrade on a cell phone, the latest fashion trend, and so on. All of these things are great to have and should be enjoyed. However, splurging on these items can be very expensive and addictive. You and I know people who absolutely have to get the upgrades each and every time they are made available. Don't fall for the marketing schemes that constantly lure you to buy things because you gotta have it.

The fourth reason people choose not to save money is that they want to live in the moment. They want to travel, take vacations, shop, and so on. Again, there's nothing wrong with doing these things. I encourage you to have a good time and enjoy everyday life. However, living in the moment doesn't mean you can't plan for the future. You can walk and chew bubblegum at the same time.

Ivory Hodges

Living in the moment doesn't mean going all in and leaving nothing out. You can still save money, but you just can't save as much money. Your financial goals will determine how you prioritize your funds. Just be aware that if you live in the moment all the time, you may have less money to set aside for the future.

Also, many young professionals who do not have children often say they don't need to save because they don't have any kids. They think that all their money is to be spent on themselves. However, there are plenty of other reasons you should be saving money: to pay off your student loans early, save for emergencies, or purchase an item with cash. You can start saving money today, without the misery, once you have a purpose behind the savings.

Did I miss anything? If so, read on.

Dare to get ready for change. Life is flying by fast. You don't have another second to waste doing the same old things. It's time to take a new direction; it's time for a new course. Change is hard, but it's not impossible. Open your mind and heart to receive transformation.

38

There are plenty of testimonies from people all over the world who have made significant changes in their lives. You may know someone who used to be overweight, and now they are able to get into a slim-fit suit or wear a fitted summer dress. My mother used to smoke cigarettes. She smoked two packs a day for eighteen years. One day she decided to kick the habit. It didn't happen overnight, but transformation took place when she set her mind toward change. Change can happen for you. You are no different from the people who get out of debt every day. I'm asking you to make the tough decision today so that your tomorrow will be much easier. You can get anywhere as long as you take one step at a time.

Part II
More Action, Less
Information

3

If Not Now, Then When?

*M*any times in life we have aspirations to do great things. We start out having ambitious life goals, but somewhere along the line, we slowly drift away from them. Maybe your goal for the year is to get out of debt, start saving for a home, or meeting with a financial adviser to discuss your retirement plan. Once you have lived a few years, you understand how precious your time really is. When you were younger, you knew there were certain things that screamed for your attention, things that needed to be done, but you were too busy or you felt like you would eventually get around to it. Besides, there was always tomorrow.

If you needed to lose a few pounds or start eating healthier foods, you could attend to that later. You knew that you needed to get some car maintenance done, but you drove the car into the ground. What could it hurt to focus on today and let the future play itself out? You were working too long, not spending enough time with your spouse and kids, but next year when you got the promotion, it would all change. You sure weren't going to live like this forever. Someday when you would get things in order, then you would pay down your debt.

Things got busy, and somehow you just didn't get around to it. It's human nature to put things off. But if you're not careful, you could find yourself living with regret. Thoughts of regret will flood your mind: *I've been working all these years, and I have little to show for it. I could have been debt-free by now.* Some people wait until the very last minute to do things. We know that we should be saving more money, managing our finances better, teaching our children about money. If you don't do it now, then when will you? Mark Twain said it this way: "Never put off tomorrow what you can do today."

I read a parable about a procrastinator. Three devils set out to conquer the world. The first devil went around proclaiming, "There is no God!" But even though some people acted as if there were no God, they knew in their hearts that this message was not true. The second devil announced, "There is no sin!" And again, although many people acted as if the message were true, they knew deep down that it wasn't. The third devil was smarter than the other two. He did not attempt to change people's beliefs. He made no attempt to argue against their deepest convictions. He simply said, "There is no hurry."

Do you feel like you have all the time in the world, that managing your money isn't a top priority at the moment? Now is the time to get serious about your future. There will always be a reason to delay what you know needs to be done.

Friends, if you don't do it now, then when will you do it? One of the key ingredients of financial success is having the courage to take action. When you make a decision to do something about your situation, that's when real change begins. The battle starts in your mind. Thoughts will come to you: *I can wait; I'm too tired; maybe next year*, but—can I tell you?—tomorrow or next year never comes. You have to put your foot down and say, "That's it;

I'm not going to go another day living beneath my privilege."

This is what Charles and Tammy did. They were newlyweds. Combined, they had about $70,000 in student-loan debt, spent every dime they made, and maxed out their credit cards; they weren't putting anything in their 401(k) accounts, and so on. They were living as if there were no tomorrow. One day, Tammy began to realize that she and her husband were making good money, but they felt they did not have adequate savings in case of an emergency. She had a discussion with her husband and shared that she didn't feel secure. Charles agreed. Just before they went to bed one night, they started talking about their future. Charles shared how he'd like to get out of debt as soon as possible so they could start putting away money for their kids' college funds.

They made a decision to work with me to help put their goals into action. Long story short, they took action on their goals, got focused on what needed to be done, and now they are well on their way to achieving financial peace of mind. Hebrews 12:11 says, "No discipline seems pleasant at the time, but painful. Later on, however, it produces a harvest of righteousness and peace for those who have been trained by it."

Your future is filled with explosive blessings! Are you sitting on the sidelines of life unsatisfied, without passion, longing for a sense of fulfillment? It's time to get your mojo back! Where you are right now isn't your financial destination. You need to say, "Enough is enough. I'm not gonna live one more day dragging through life without moving toward a brighter future." The question is, "Are you willing to do what it takes today in order to win tomorrow?"

You have the opportunity to change your family tree. You have a golden opportunity to leave a solid legacy for your children's children. If you wait for the perfect conditions, you will never get anything done. President Obama said, "Change will not come if we wait for some other person or some other time. We are the ones we've been waiting for. We are the change that we seek."

I knew a man by the name of Lawrence. He found himself drowning in debt a few years ago. Lawrence comes from a poor family with very limited resources. Life was stressful for a long time. Lawrence worked two jobs just to make ends meet. He knew that there had to be a better way. He was consistently living paycheck to paycheck and sometimes found himself borrowing money from friends and family just to make it to the next month. Lawrence got sick and tired of being sick and tired. One day he decided to do what I'm asking you to do. He decided to take action now instead of waiting for something or someone else.

It didn't happen overnight, but he was able to focus on the things that mattered to him and where he wanted to be in the short and long run. He made provisions to get on a sensible spending plan to eliminate all his debts in a little over two years while supporting his wife and two kids. He did it by cutting up his credit cards, eliminating nonessential expenses (like cable TV), sticking to a budget, and increasing his income. Lawrence has been debt-free since that time and is now maxing out his 401(k). He told me that he has plans to pay off his thirty-year mortgage in just eight years!

Some of you are going through difficult financial times or even crisis today. Maybe you went through a divorce or a job loss, and you're wondering how you are going to make it. Your income might not be enough to cover your expenses, but the bill collectors keep calling. When you have a financial plan and you are actively working through it, you won't ignore those bill collectors, thinking, *I'll never get out of debt.* No, instead you'll run to them knowing that you have a financial plan to get rid of them once and for all. You won't run away from working extra hours, or taking a part-time job, thinking, *What's the point?* You'll run toward it knowing that you're getting closer to having financial peace of mind. Friends, incredible power is released when we believe we can do anything we set our minds to. I'm asking you to get rid of the negative thoughts that say things like "I'll always be broke," "I'll always be in debt," or "I'm not qualified to be in management." No one can stop you from reaching your fullest potential except you.

One day I was at McDonald's reading a book about personal finance for twentysomethings. As I was minding my own business and taking pleasure in my book, a guy named Paul walked up to me, tapped me on the shoulder, and asked if he could talk with me for a few minutes. I wasn't in a hurry, so I stopped what I was doing to chat with him. He was very excited about the book I was reading. We started having a discussion about the book, our own personal goals and plans, and the dreams we wanted to accomplish. He told me he was burdened with student-loan and credit-card debt. Combined, he had racked up $55,000 in the blink of an eye.

He shared how he dreamed of the day when he could scream that he was completely debt-free. I asked him when he thought he would reach his goal. He said he was on track to be completely debt-free, of both student loans and credit-card debt, within the next few months. It took him only three years to pay off $55,000!

You may ask, "How in the world did he do that?" I wasn't surprised because I knew that the decision to do something like that would take discipline and sacrifice, but most importantly, a made-up mind to take action. We exchanged contact information, and I told him to let me know when he had completed his goal of becoming debt-free. Several months later, he sent me a video explaining how he had finally reached his goals.

At just twenty-seven years old, Paul is well on his way to living a life of financial peace. Now imagine with me, just how many people can he help? How much faster can he build wealth now that he has freed up his money and is no longer making payments? Paul isn't any different from you. He worked hard, made tough sacrifices, and had a mind-set to be free. You have what it takes to reach your financial goals, as well. You may say, "Ivory, I'm behind on my bills, and I don't even make enough money to do anything." Author Zig Ziglar said, "Everybody wants the same things—to be happy, to be healthy, to be at least reasonably prosperous, and to be secure. They want friends, peace of mind, good family relationships, and hope that tomorrow is going to be even better than today." The question is, "Are you willing to fight for it?" How bad do you want it? If you get your thoughts going in the right direction, your life tends to follow suit. Again, the battle starts in your mind.

I remember talking to a man who was down on life. He was extremely depressed. At one point in his life, he had contemplated suicide. He told me he had lost his passion for life and didn't have much to live for. As we were talking, he went on and on, telling me about his problems, explaining in dramatic detail all the bad luck he'd had and saying how crazy it was and how impossible it looked. He was good at talking about all his problems. I told him what I'm telling you. You've got to start believing that your future is bright and be willing to fight for it. Your blessings are on the other side of action.

You've got to start putting positivity into your mind and heart. I encouraged him to go through the day saying things like "I'm blessed. I am a good father; debt and depression are only temporary. I am a victor!" I saw him about nine months later, and he was filled with joy! He told me he had started speaking words of faith and focusing on his purpose. He told me he had started a nonprofit organization to help people overcome depression. He said, "Ivory, I allowed doubt and guilt to dictate my life. I've been dead for the last ten years, but now I'm alive and walking in my destiny. I'm at peace with myself, and I'm living a prosperous life." I believe he would still be in deep depression or maybe even have committed suicide if he had not gotten rid of the negative thoughts and started doing something about his situation.

Words alone won't solve your problems. You have to follow up with strategic action, or you could get stuck. Understand that one of the first steps to doing something about your financial situation is to identify what your financial-stress buttons are. For many people, these buttons could be worries about debt, paying bills late, not having financial security, not having a sense of control over your finances, or having arguments about money. I want to give you some simple yet powerful solutions to each of those buttons.

If you're going to get out of debt, you have to stop borrowing money. You cannot borrow your way out of debt. It's so easy to get into debt but much harder to get out. Pay attention to your impulse-spending urges to stop the bleeding. Pay your bills as soon as they come in. This is one of the easiest ways to eliminate stress over bills. When you get your electric bill, go to your computer, log in, and send your electronic payment. To do this, you'll need to develop a bit of a cushion in your bank account, so you always have enough to pay the bills as they come in.

Once you get into the swing of things, I highly recommend making your payments automatic. It's a great alternative to having to mail in your payment. You won't even have to think about it; the payment amount is automatically taken out for you. Also, review your finances at least quarterly. To get a sense of control over your finances, you have to monitor them. Even if your bills are automatic, you'll still want to make sure they're going out. Take ten to twenty minutes each pay period to look at your budget, your expenses, and your income, and make sure you've got everything under control. If you have a spouse, do this together.

Money can be a huge stressor in a relationship. It's important that you talk about money on a regular basis in a nonemotional way, as hard as that may sound. It's crucial, in fact, to the survival of your relationship. You both have to be on the same page, or you will eventually argue and have major crises about your finances. You need to talk about your financial dreams and goals; your spending patterns; your budget; your income; and your savings, debts, bills, and the like. If you don't already do these things, it may take a while in the beginning, and it may be difficult. But try to do it as a team and not accuse each other of anything. Don't blame, and try to be positive and constructive. Over time, it will get easier.

If you're single, find someone you trust and ask them to be your accountability partner.

Some of you are praying about things you have the power to do something about now. My challenge to you is to start doing something about it. You have prayed about it long enough. Set your mind to getting things in order. If you do this, you will experience the peace you've long desired. Just like Lawrence, Paul, and Charles and Tammy, you will overcome obstacles that look permanent. You will accomplish dreams you thought were not possible, and I believe you will reach your fullest potential!

4

Motion Creates Emotion

We might be blessed in many areas of our lives, such as having good jobs, excellent health, loving families, and so on. There are days when life seems as pleasant as a sunny, warm day on the beach. But then there are times when it's hard even to get out of bed. Every now and then, you just don't feel like doing anything. Sometimes you may lack motivation for no apparent reason. Maybe you had financial goals, but then you had an experience with the great teacher called "life," and now you feel flat, stressed, and worried. The spring in your step has rusted out, and now there's a sense of boredom and heaviness. You long for inspiration and passion to ignite you. All you want to do is feel a little bit better about your current situation.

We all go through the ups and downs of life; some of us respond better than others. Maybe you were on the right track; you had your financial house in order—paying all your bills on time and consistently saving money, but you lost your job, and everything came crashing down. Or maybe you always lived on the edge and now live from paycheck to paycheck. One simple change today can make all the difference in the world.

If you are having a difficult time gaining traction with your financial goals, one of the simplest things you can do is to get your "hope and passion" tank refilled. One Saturday night, a few friends and I went salsa dancing. One of our friends had just come out of a difficult breakup a few days earlier. He wasn't in the mood for anything. He would wake up depressed, wishing that night would come quickly, and he would go to bed wishing that daytime would soon arrive. We asked him if he wanted to go out with us. He quickly said no; he wanted to be alone. Eventually we convinced him to go with us. When we arrived at the dancing event, my friend Joe seemed uninterested and detached. The rest of us were having a great time laughing, dancing, and mingling with other people while Joe just sat there and watched. As the night went on, one of the salsa dancers grabbed Joe by the hand and twirled him around a few times. The crowd began to form a circle around the two. The music was going; the crowd was engaged; and Joe was participating. After that quick dance, everyone in the crowd applauded very loudly.

The fun and excitement actually compelled Joe to get up from where he was despite how he felt. After the first dance, Joe started talking and laughing with us again. A few minutes later, he was leading a *Soul Train* line! By the end of the night, Joe was fully engaged and was the life of the party! I'd never seen him so free and full of life. He thanked us for inviting him out.

A few days later, I called Joe to see how he was doing. He told me that the night of salsa dancing was a turning point for him. That night, he made a conscious decision to be happy and move on with his life. During the following weeks, I definitely could see the changes taking place within Joe. He told me he was going to focus on becoming a better person each day. He also started going back to the gym and playing his guitar, and after several months, he even began dating again.

So, what happened? Joe was refilling his "hope and passion" tank. He started living life again. He shifted to a place where his self-worth wasn't tied to external forces. Once he got moving, the fire within him was ignited. The takeaway lesson is that you have to make a move! That's exactly what Joe did. Something as simple as a dance sparked positive change in Joe's life. Positive emotions can get you going!

In the same way, with your finances, you may have had a few setbacks. Maybe you finished school, and now you have tons of student-loan debt. You're wondering how in the world you are going to pay it all off. Or maybe you lost your home and had to start from ground zero. You might have suffered other financial pains like filing for bankruptcy or the effects of a divorce. Whatever hindrances you've faced or are currently facing, they will not last forever. All you need is a few small wins to boost your momentum. Creating a budget is a small win. Opening a retirement account is a small win. Sharing your financial goals with a trusted person is a small win. There are plenty of ways to start building momentum, and once the ball gets rolling, it gets bigger and bigger.

My oldest nephew is a creative kid. He enjoys working with his hands. One of his favorite things to do during the wintertime is to create snowmen. The first snowman we made was a thing of art! Normally, my nephew and I would make the snowman together. But this time he wanted to make his own. He couldn't get the snowball to get bigger. He tried and tried a few times, but he wasn't making much progress. As I was standing by, watching him, I noticed how he became so frustrated that he wanted to give up. I got the process started for him by forming a small ball. He was excited! All he needed was a jump start. Now he could begin to work on his snowman. I went inside the house to make us some hot cocoa. About ten minutes later, my nephew had turned the small snowball into a huge snow boulder! That year, he made the largest snowman in his neighborhood.

What am I saying? Sometimes all you need is a little push. You need a lighter to set off your match. As you start filling your "hope and passion" tank, you will begin to build some serious momentum. Imagine what you could do if you had a full tank of hope and passion, and you aimed it directly at your debt. Imagine how fast you could build savings if you didn't have to make debt payments. How much more could you give to charity? How would working together as a team improve your marriage? I've started your mini hope-and-passion snowball. Now, add to it.

Maybe you want to start saving money for emergencies. Do you have something that you are no longer using that could be sold for cash? Have you considered having a garage sale? If so, then set the date, and get it done! This applies to your career as well. There are ways to start accelerating toward the next level. Instead of listening to work gossip at the watercooler, listen to recordings from industry leaders, or read a few pages of a nonfiction book in your line of work. Building yourself up is a sure way to gain the insight needed to thrust yourself forward. Throughout this book, I have stressed taking action. Life is flying by! You don't have time to sit on the sidelines, nursing wounds. Whatever you are going to do in this lifetime, start doing it now because once you're gone, it's too late!

Procrastination is our biggest enemy. One of the best ways you can fight procrastination is to get moving on what you know you need to do. Find someone to be your accountability partner. I remember when I was desperately trying to lose weight. I dreaded going to the gym, and when I did go, I didn't give it my full effort. I was simply going through the motions. I have a friend named Tiffany who is a health and fitness nut. Tiffany was in much better shape than I was. During that time, she was training for a bodybuilding competition. She was very diligent with her food selections and intake portions. She also went to the gym five or six days a week! Her body was chiseled. I asked her to be my accountability partner. She agreed. I gave her permission to hurt my feelings and to kick my butt if I started slacking off. I gave her my fitness goals, and, boy, did she hold me accountable to them! There were days when I felt like pigging out at the all-you-can-eat restaurants. And sure enough, Tiffany would text me and ask if I was staying true to my goals. Sometimes, I could hear her voice in the back of my mind when I was thinking of quitting. I was strengthened by her zeal for fitness. Eventually, I was able to drop the weight and change my eating habits. Tiffany was instrumental in helping me reach my fitness goals. She kept me on my toes and provided the extra push I needed to go further when I was at a standstill.

You can do the same thing by working toward the things that will help you reach your highest potential and enjoy everyday life. Is there someone you can trust to hold you accountable to your goals? Find someone who will be completely honest and give you direct feedback. The best way to change your financial circumstances is to get moving with a plan. Start doing what you know you need to do, and good things will follow. I encourage you to start thinking about something that will motivate you to get moving. As you fill up your "hope and passion" tank, you will have what you need to finish your financial race.

5

Further Faster

You may be thinking, *How in the world I will get out of debt?* Or maybe you are getting closer to retirement, and you know that you don't have enough saved to leave your profession. It's easy to stay where you are and settle for second best. But the good news is that you can do something about your financial situation. Having solid financial goals that are clear and concise will motivate you to move forward. When we have financial goals, we are more likely to stay focused. When you get your tax refund, instead of going down to the mall and buying a new flat-screen TV, your goals will take priority. If you don't have concrete financial goals, I have work sheets in the back of this book that will help you develop SMART financial goals (specific, measurable, achievable, realistic, and time bound).

You cannot hit a target that you cannot see. Setting SMART goals is one of the most powerful ways to accomplish your goals in a fraction of the time. Let's say you want to get in shape for the summer, but you don't know where to start. You first need to start with a well-defined goal. Instead of saying, *I want to get in shape*, your goal might be *I am going to the gym three times a week, and eating less than twelve hundred calories for ninety days*. Studies have shown that specific plans have a greater chance of being carried out than general goals.

Many people have a vague sense of what they desire. They have a general sense of what they want, but it's not a clear goal. When you start setting SMART goals, keep the five "W" questions in mind: who, what, when, where, and why. These questions will allow you to hone in on what exactly it is you're trying to accomplish. If you are paying the minimum balance on your credit cards, student loans, and so on, it will take you forever to pay off the entire balance. If getting out of debt is one of your goals, you can get further faster with the power of focus. You are one shift away from creating the synergy needed to break out. What am I talking about? Getting out of debt is more emotional than it is about math. You need to stay pumped up and motivated. When you see a small debt paid off, you will be encouraged to keep going.

Let's go through an example of how an effective SMART goal can help you move the needle. Say that Jeff was a recent college graduate and he had $20,000 in student-loan debt. Virtually everyone who ever had student loans knows how annoying they can be, especially when you have to make the payment every month. But there's a huge difference between saying, "I want to get out of debt" (generic) and "I want to pay off $20,000 in student loans in thirty-six months by saving $600 a month" (specific). Now that Jeff has a specific amount to pay off, he can measure his progress every time he makes a payment toward the debt.

That way, Jeff will stay pumped up about paying off his student loans. Also, it's important to have a way of measuring your progress (measurable). You might use the debt snowball. I will explain how you can use the debt-snowball technique to totally eliminate all your debts in an explosive way!

Let's go back to our example with Jeff. Now that Jeff has a specific and measurable goal, the question becomes "Is that goal attainable?" An attainable goal is something within reach and not too difficult to achieve. Now, it would be very difficult if Jeff didn't have any income, and his goal was to get out of debt in six months. Next is being "realistic": Can Jeff pay $600 a month toward his student-loan debt? Can Jeff really pay off $20,000 in student loans in thirty-six months by saving $600 a month? Several factors will have to be taken into consideration. Is Jeff willing to sacrifice today in order to win tomorrow? What happens when Jeff is tempted to use the extra student-loan payment for a new item he wants? Will Jeff need to increase his income, decrease his spending, or both? As you can see, a lot will depend on his income, responsibilities, expenses, and, most importantly, his level of intensity!

Now, if he's making $2,000 a month with a child, paying $850 in rent, making a car payment of $350, and has utility bills, and so on, this may be an unrealistic goal based on his income. But if Jeff is bringing home $5,000 a month, and he doesn't have any kids, and his expenses are relatively low, this can be a realistic goal. The next letter is "T" for "time bound." Every goal has to have an end date. A goal without an ending is a dream. Again, goals need deadlines so that you will stay focused and motivated.

In our example with Jeff, he decides to pay off his $20,000 student-loan debt by paying $600 a month for about thirty-six months. There's something about deadlines that makes people switch into overdrive and take action. You will also want your time frame to be flexible so that you won't get discouraged if you don't reach your goal within a certain time frame. It's OK to give yourself some grace by having a ballpark estimate of when you plan to arrive at your goal.

Now that we have gone through an example of what a SMART goal looks like, I want to show you another way to move further faster by paying down your debts. Here's how the debt snowball can help you get out of debt in far less time than you think. I love the debt-snowball technique. It has been around for a long time and has helped thousands of people get out of debt. When my nephew was making a large snowball, we did it by packing snow into a really tight ball so we would have a foundation to build upon. Then we started rolling it through the backyard. By the time we rolled it to the front of the yard, our snowball had become a huge snow boulder. It would have taken a longer time to build the snowball up by hand. The debt-snowball technique works the same way. I hope you are getting excited! Shall we continue?

Before starting your debt snowball, you should be current on all your bills. Also, you should have a starter emergency fund set aside. I recommend having anywhere from $1,000 to $5,000 for your starter emergency fund. By having a mini emergency fund, you should be able to reduce little emergencies to mere inconveniences. This will allow you to focus all your firepower on your debts, and if an emergency does come up, you will have a cushion to deal with it without disrupting your debt-elimination plan.

Now, back to the debt snowball. Assuming all your debt is current or easily made current, this technique calls for all your nonmortgage debt to be prioritized, from smallest balance to largest balance. Don't worry about interest rates. We don't care if one debt has a 4 percent interest rate and another has a 25 percent interest rate. Make minimum payments on all debts except the smallest one, and attack the smallest one with a vengeance! As that debt is paid off, those payments are rolled forward into the next smallest balance, plus any extra money you can muster up, and attack the next debt on the list. Once that one is gone, take the combined payment and go to the next debt on the list. Keep knocking those bad boys out, one by one, until they are all gone!

For those of you who are visual learners, there's a cool YouTube video by Countryside Christian Center (go to YouTube and type debt snowball method and look for Countryside Christian Center video) about how the debt-snowball method works.

For the rest of us, let's work through an example.

Let's say you have the following debts:

- $200 department-store credit card ($25 payment)
- $1,000 Visa credit—card debt ($50 payment)
- $10,000 car-loan balance ($184 payment)
- $15,000 student-loan balance ($172 payment)

Now that we have our list of debts in order from smallest to largest, you would start making minimum payments on everything except the department credit card. For this example, let's say you find an extra five hundred bucks each month by working overtime, cutting back on your lifestyle, or working a part-time job, and so on. Since you are paying $25 a month and have $500 a month to work with, that department credit card is immediately paid off! Now, take that $525 and hit the Visa credit card. You will be paying $575 on the Visa credit card (the freed-up $525 plus the $50 Visa minimum payment). In about two months, kick your credit-card debt to the curb! It is paid off in full!

Now, let's get to work on the car loan. You are pumped up and have that snowball rolling! Instead of paying the regular car payment of $184 a month, you will be paying $759 a month. In just thirteen months, you can do the happy dance. Now the snowball is getting even bigger! Now, it's time to put all your aim and firepower on the last payment: the student loan. You will be throwing $931 ($500 + $25 + $50 + $184 + $172 = $931) a month toward it. It will only last about fifteen months! After that, you can do your ultimate happy dance! All the hard work and self-denial will have paid off! You will have paid off $26,200 in only thirty-one months using the debt-snowball technique! You did it! Yes, it will take some discipline and intensity in order to get out of debt.

Behavioral change is the biggest point of the debt snowball. Well, you may say, "Ivory, why not start paying the student loan first because it's the largest debt?" If you started with the student loan, it would take a while before you paid it off. This is a fast way to lose momentum and eventually stop making extra payments and still have those annoying debts around your neck. However, when you knock out the smallest debt first, you see progress and start catching fire. Now you're ready to kill the next one and then the next one. It's just like losing weight. Once you see that the plan is working, you'll stick with it. You will build huge momentum that causes you to modify your behavior. You are paying a lot more of your debt off at once instead of a little bit here and there. By the time you are paying down your larger debts, you will have a lot of money freed up from paying off the earlier debts, so it will cause a huge snowball to result. It is easy to see how you can start paying off some serious debt in no time!

Congratulations! You've made it! You paid off your debts; now what? Remember that starter emergency fund of $1,000 to $5,000? Now it's time to increase that amount to cover three to nine months of expenses. This should take a relatively shorter amount of time because you have no payments. Let's say that your monthly expenses are $3,000 a month. That means you would want to save anywhere from $9,000 to $27,000 (three to nine months' expenses).

After establishing your full emergency fund, now would be the time to start saving to purchase a vehicle, to make a down payment on a home, or to start investing in your retirement account and college fund for the kids. At this point, you won't have payments, and you will have already gotten into the habit of saving money. You will have what it takes to live the life you want. After reading this chapter, I hope you will see yourself as a champion. You have the information and the motivation. Action is the last ingredient to add to the mix. The deeper the sacrifice, the faster you get out of debt and the higher the probability you will reach your financial goals.

Part III
Commit to the Cause

6

Changing Your Family Tree

Over the years, I have coached dozens of clients who wanted to make changes with managing their money. They would get so pumped up about their new financial plans, they were about to burst into the clouds. But what happens when you are having trouble getting your spouse on board with the plan? How do you deal with a spouse who isn't involved with the finances or who is reluctant to work with you? Sometimes, it can be very difficult for a couple to get on the same page and mutually agree on a plan moving forward. Money fights and money problems constitute the number-one cause of divorce in America. One reason these issues come up so frequently is that couples don't have discussions before they get married about their views on finances, what they envision their financial futures to be, their needs versus their wants, and so on. Having the money talk doesn't come naturally. Few parents teach their children the values and principles of money management. When two people come together as a couple, they are often coming from opposite sides regarding money. One spouse might be a spender while the other is a penny pincher. Too often, couples fight about money because there isn't mutual agreement or direction for how their finances will be handled. There are many areas where a couple doesn't see eye to eye, but I want to shed light on two of the most explosive areas when dealing with finances.

Here's an example of a typical couple arguing about spending: Spouse A went to the local department store and purchased a relatively expensive laptop computer. However, spouse A was able to find a coupon online, and there was an in-store discount as well. This was an offer that was just too good to be true! Spouse A believed he or she needed the item, and plus he or she was able to get a really good deal on it as well. The issue is that spouse A never discussed the purchase with spouse

B until it showed up on their debit-card statement. Oops! Now we've got a fight on our hands. The name-calling, shouting match and fussing begins. This is no way to live. How can you find a happy medium in your relationship without allowing relationship problems to explode? Will savers and spenders ever unite?

One spouse might be the coupon-cutting, super-saving penny pincher while the other is a free-spirited spender with no regard for the details. The saver might point the finger at the spender and say that they are the problem. The spender may tell off the saver by saying how they need to "chill out" and "have some fun." Yes, it's true; savers can be a little bit stubborn. (I admit I am a saver!) But oftentimes, they have the family's long-term financial well-being and emergency preparedness in mind. The spender gets a bad rap and is labeled irresponsible. However, the spender prefers the short-term enjoyment that spending money can bring. They often bring the fun and spontaneity, which makes for great experiences. The key to having financial peace and unity in your relationship is compromising and working together.

Marriage is the ultimate team sport. You may love your spouse but hate the way they handle money. If you don't work together for the greater good, you risk the chance of getting stuck and opening a backdoor for resentment and bitterness to take root. In order to tackle the problem at its core, couples need to understand that they BOTH spend money; however, they spend it differently. Generally speaking, men spend money on big-ticket items like cars, electronics, and so on while women spend money on clothes, family and household needs, food, the bills, and so on. This difference in spending sometimes can be misconstrued, leading to false perceptions.

Here's the key: when you sit down and have a "managing money with my honey date": code word for "budget," *both* partners must be involved with the cash-flow plan. The administrative spouse can prepare the budget, but the decision making must be done by both spouses. Work together to maximize wisdom: two heads are better than one. This will help prevent so many money fights and bring unity to the relationship. There's nothing wrong with compromising for the overall good of the relationship, but don't allow yourself to be a punching bag either!

Debt also can be an area where couples can have disagreement. In our culture, most couples enter the relationship with some form of debt. Whether it's student loans, a mortgage, a car loan, or credit-card debt, one or both spouses may be carrying some sort of financial baggage. To make matters worse, what if one spouse enters the marriage with a significantly larger amount of debt than the other? Unless the debt was hidden, it isn't helpful pointing a finger at the spouse with the most debt. My mother used to say that once you are married, what's yours becomes mine and vice versa—that includes debt! Instead, consider working together as a team to knock it out once and for all.

Both spouses need to be on board about these issues in a reasonable way. Having open and honest communication and trying to understand your spouse's point of view is the best way to proceed. If you are dating and plan to get married, it's extremely important to know your spouse's debt loads. This is essential so that you know exactly what you are getting into. It's OK to plan for the wedding, but make sure you invest some time into money discussions as well. Debt can have a huge impact on a relationship, especially when there's no plan in place to get rid of it. If you don't have a plan in place, start by focusing on solutions not just the problems. As you start to focus on solutions, you will begin to see subtle changes for the better.

Your relationship goes to a whole new level when you drop your need to get your way in every battle. Imagine how much further you can go by creating shared goals instead of individual ambitions. Happy relationships are developed by giving up selfish desires in order to win together. Jesus, the master teacher, said that a house divided against itself cannot stand. Remember that you are on the same team. Working together will propel your relationship to the next level. You will get further down the road faster, and you will be able to teach your children how to handle money in a way that unites the family. Your family legacy can be passed on from generation to generation.

Let's not forget about the children! Proverbs 22:6 says, "Point your kids in the right direction—when they are old they won't be lost." Believe it or not, your children are paying attention to you. They are like little sponges. It's important to teach them how to properly manage money and be responsible. Children primarily learn about money management from their parents. It makes all the difference in the world when they see parents in sync with each other. Whatever age children are, it's never too early or too late to start teaching them solid money-management skills. When you have your financial house in order and are teaching your children about money, you are changing your family tree. You are preparing the next generation to be better off than you were.

7

Life Is Complicated; Your Finances Don't Have to Be

Ever found yourself looking at the calendar, realizing you have eight days until the next paycheck and wondering how in the world you are going to make it until next week? You borrowed money from family, friends, or coworkers with good intentions of paying them back. But since you paid a few bills late, you were charged with penalties and late fees, not to mention the money you spend here and there on coffee, gas, and lunch. Eight days finally pass, and payday has arrived! Yay! But guess what? You have to pay back those folks you borrowed money from. More bills are due; emergency situations come up, and before you know it, a special event for a friend or family member comes out of the blue. What do you do?

In most cases, the cycle of financial drama continues to play out. This is an unhealthy way to live.

When your finances are out of whack, you add unnecessary pressure on yourself. In the back of your mind, you hope you haven't spent the mortgage money on the groceries you've just purchased.

The good news is that you don't have to live your life hoping, wishing, and praying that everything works out. You have more control over your finances than you think. One of the first things you have to do is be truthful with yourself. You have to put your foot down and say, "That's it! I've had enough of this!" If you aren't mad enough about your situation, nothing will change. I've learned that the people who are most likely to succeed in changing their financial behaviors are the ones who acknowledge the truth and take small action steps. They use this emotional energy to work to their advantage. Instead of making excuses, they say things like "I hate paying the minimum balance on my credit-card bill. Next month I'm going to pay the balance in full and stick to my budget for the month." They may take an action step by developing a realistic budget to help them stay focused on the goal of paying the full credit-card balance.

Well, you say, "Ivory, I don't like doing budgets; I don't have the time to do a budget, and I do my budget in my head." Today, life is too busy, and if we are not careful, things will slip our minds. A good friend of mine who's a lawyer says that if you don't write it down, it never happened. The truth is you can't afford not to do a budget. A failure to plan is a plan to fail. A budget is simply planning how you will spend your money. If you don't tell your money where to go, you will wonder where it went. I've coached hundreds of people, and during my sessions I often heard people say things like "Do I have to do a budget?" with a little whine in their voices.

Today in America, we have a lot of people spending more than they make and covering the difference by using credit cards. Imagine having a monthly spending plan in place that allows you to be in control of your finances, spend less than you make, and save more for rainy days—how much easier would life be? In order to do this, you will have to build discipline with a little sacrifice by paying yourself first and doing a budget every month, before the month begins. We all know that we should be saving for emergencies. After all, cars do break down; people get sick; accidents happen.

From my experience, here are the top five reasons people don't budget. You may find yourself guilty of one of them. The number-one excuse people make for not budgeting is they think budgeting is too complicated and time-consuming. This couldn't be further from the truth. Actually, budgeting isn't complicated at all, especially if you are leveraging technology. There are tons of apps and software you can used to develop a realistic budget. Even if you're old school (pen and notepad), you can write down what you have coming in, what expenses you have going out, and then plan accordingly. On average, it takes me about fifteen to twenty minutes to lay out my budget for the entire month. That's less time than it takes to wait in the coffee drive-through every morning, shorter than the average commute to work, and about the same amount of time as it takes to get car insurance from Geico! If you are new to budgeting, it may take you a little bit longer during the first few months because it takes getting used to laying out income and expenses along with looking at your calendar for upcoming events. But budgeting your money isn't rocket science.

The second reason many people don't like budgeting is that they say they don't have the time to do it. Don't fall into the trap of telling yourself that you don't have time to do a budget. We make time for what we want to do. Why not make time to plan how you will spend your hard-earned money? Research suggests that the average American will have more than a million dollars pass through their hands during their working lifetime. Don't you owe it to yourself to be responsible with that kind of money?

I read a story about a successful basketball player. He had earned over $123 million during his career as a basketball player, and now he is bankrupt. I'm sure he had good intentions for managing his money properly. The famous basketball player said that he always lived in the moment and never thought that his money was going to dry up. It is especially dangerous when you have no sense of direction about where the money is going.

Generally speaking, most people don't expect their income to dry up. They are hopeful that they won't be laid off or that somehow they can count on a certain amount every time. The bottom line is that you can find the time to complete your monthly budget if you make time to do it. If you'll commit to planning, your life will get that much easier.

The third reason people don't budget is because of emotional spending and stress. Generally speaking, weekends can be the times when budgets are blown. After a long workweek, you may want to just go out and have a good time. Parties, gatherings, sporting events, bars, and local attractions are great places to have fun. However, if we are not careful, we could find ourselves overspending without even realizing it.

I've done this plenty of times. When I first started budgeting, I made plenty of mistakes. Throughout the weekdays I would be just fine, sticking with my budget without any problems. On the weekends, there was always something going on, and there was no way I was going to deprive myself of having fun. I would go out and have so much fun living in the moment. It got so bad that I started leaving my debit card at home because I would swipe my card and forget to track my spending, and on top of that, those funds had already been set aside for something else. I needed to learn how to have some pocket money without overspending. Eventually I learned that all I needed to do was tweak my budget and set aside "blow money." The blow money allowed me to do whatever I wanted (within reason) without being accountable. The set amount of money would allow me to spend however I wanted to. If I wanted to blow it on random items or impulse, I would simply spend the money without feeling guilty afterward. Don't allow stress and emotion to keep you from developing and sticking to your budget.

The fourth reason people don't budget their money is because of convenience. Let's face it. Without convenience, life would be so inconvenient! How handy is it to grab your phone and get an Uber ride whenever you need one? No big deal, but when you're paying for convenience all the time, you won't be able to remember where your money is going. All I'm saying is that we should be aware of the impact of convenience. Grabbing a cup of coffee from Starbucks every morning can add up pretty fast if you're not careful. It can easily cause you to blow your budget.

One of the best and easiest ways to curb over-spending is to use the envelope system. Suppose you are budgeting and have been diligently doing so for some time. Yet every month, you overspend. Sure, you took the time to do your budget, and you have good intentions about sticking to it. The question is, "What can hold you accountable to that budget?" The envelope system is an easy way to control spending. Yes, it does require carry-ing some cash, but the benefits far outweigh the inconvenience. When you run out of funds in your envelope, you stop spending. It is as simple as that. Another good thing about the envelope system is that you don't have to save up any money to start. You can start today with the money you have today.

Here is how the process works. Let's walk through an example. Suppose you have budgeted $200 a month for restaurants. Today is payday. You would take $200 out and put the cash in an envelope marked "Restaurants." In order to build discipline, you would only use this money to pay for restaurants and nothing more. No cheating! So when you have the urge to go out to eat, simply look in your restaurant envelope, and if there's money available, you go. But once you have spent all $200, you can't go to any more restaurants until next month. Besides, there's nothing wrong with eating leftovers. If you have money left over in your restaurant envelope at the end of the month, great. You can roll that money over so you will have more in your restaurant budget for the next month. Or you can use it to celebrate your victory. It's important to celebrate your victories and reward yourself so that you can continue with the momentum you've built.

Here are some pointers I've learned from experience to keep you on track with the envelope system. Be careful not to borrow from your other envelopes. When I first started using the envelope system, it took some getting used to. I was the biggest cheater. I basically didn't have any financial discipline. I used to take money from my clothing envelope to fund the restaurant tab when I ran out of restaurant funds. Again, the purpose of the envelope system is to keep your spending in check and build the discipline necessary for behavior change.

Here's another tip: meal planning saved me a ton of money, especially when I didn't have the money for restaurants in my envelope. There's nothing wrong with having leftovers instead of going out to eat. I know it will be tempting to cheat, especially on the weekends and special occasions. If you are in a relationship, talk with your partner to figure out what works best. You may need to adjust your envelopes based on the activities the two of you like to participate in. The most important thing is to be in agreement.

Budgeting and using the envelope system takes practice! It may take you up to three months before you start to get the hang of things. You may feel overwhelmed and frustrated after the first month of budgeting. Don't give up; keep at it, and you will start to get a feel for where your money is going. The second month will be much better. You may still have some bumps on the road, but keep at it. You are a lot further along that you realize. In the third month, you should have a solid grasp of the process and how much is coming in and going out. You will feel that sense of control and motivation to keep going. Budgeting, along with the envelope system, becomes part of your life, and it will keep you organized.

I will continue to stress the fact that you only have one life to live. Organizing your finances will bring a sense of peace and stability that will assist you in living the best life possible. There are plenty of excuses not to budget, save, or prioritize spending. If you have not been managing your money well, if you are tired of living paycheck to paycheck and wondering where your money is going, then today can be the day you make a change. I'm challenging you to start right now! Friends, your destiny is too great! Your time is too valuable. If you're going to be all that you can be, you've got to push yourself to do the uncomfortable. If you will do what you know to do, I believe that you will get to that place of rest in your finances.

8

Live Like a Champion

What do LeBron James, Tom Brady, Tiger Woods, Babe Ruth, and Serena Williams all have in common? Yes, they are champions and have plenty of accomplishments under their belts. But what they have in common is not so common, after all. Whether it was during practice, studying film, or training, they are or were always performing on a championship level. They knew they were champions long before they ever won championships. They would often fantasize about what winning would look like. They were grounded in the fact that nothing was going to stand in their way. They had to put the work, time, and energy into reaching their goals. Just like those athletes, we have to picture ourselves as champions long before the mortgage is paid off, the promotion at work, and so on. And not only this, but we have to put the time and energy into doing what it takes to manifest the success we envision.

Living like a champion requires a certain mind-set. Champions realize that the number-one enemy to their success isn't the opponent; it isn't their circumstances; it's their own thinking. You must make it a habit to control those negative thoughts that come to corrupt your mind. You may hear thoughts like *I'm not good enough*, *I don't have what it takes*, and *It's never going to happen for me*.

When those thoughts of defeat enter your mind, turn them around with positive words, even if there's no emotion. Ever heard of the saying, "Fake it till you make it"? Living like a champion requires replacing old, negative thoughts with new thoughts and new information.

Growing up, I was a huge fan of Michael Jordan. I watched all of his basketball games and wore his jerseys and shoes. Jordan was arguably the greatest basketball player of all time. While in the tenth grade, he tried out for the varsity-basketball team, but since he was five feet ten, the coaches thought he was too short to play at that level. In his sophomore year of high school, he was cut from the high-school varsity-basketball team. I'm sure thoughts like these came into his head: *You're too small. You're not good enough. You should just quit.*

But he knew deep down inside he was a champion. He was motivated to prove his worth. He trained hard and got better in every way. Years later, we all know the rest is history.

Some of us know deep down inside that we are destined to do great things, but maybe like Jordan, you were overlooked. Or maybe you were constantly told it can't be done. Or you were talked down from stepping outside the norm. If you're not careful, people will keep you from reaching your destiny. Some folks don't mean any harm by it, but they are only speaking from the experiences they've had. You can't let their experiences dictate whether you are going to become all that God has created you to be. Seeds of greatness have been sown deep down inside of us. It's no coincidence that you think the way you do or see value in things others may not see. You were created with a purpose in mind.

I've learned that nothing in life happens to you. It happens for you. What you have inside you will be brought out when you have the opportunity to be challenged. I read a story about a woman named Gerry Arrowood. She was a cake baker and had a passion for cooking. She got a job on the side helping to sell cookware. She was shy and intimidated and didn't like to be in front of people. One day her boss wasn't able to do a demonstration of the cookware to a group of people who were expecting the cookware to be delivered with a demonstration, so he asked Gerry to do it. Terror appeared in her eyes. She shook her head and said, "I just can't do it." I'm sure thoughts began to flood her mind and tell her, *You're going to make a fool out of yourself; no one will buy from you,* and *what if you forget to mention something?*

This was Gerry's most challenging moment. When it was time to deliver the cookware to the guest, something within Gerry began to rise up and what was inside her came out. The next morning Gerry was excited to tell her boss how well the demonstration had gone. Gerry told him about the fun she'd had and how pleasant it was. What happened to Gerry? A match was lit inside her. It didn't happen that day, that week, or that year, but less than five years later, Gerry Arrowood became international vice president of sales training for a multimillion-dollar cosmetics company.

The battlefield starts in your mind. Get your thoughts going in the right direction, and your mind will follow. My friend Sarah understood this principle. Sarah is smart, articulate, and informative. She is very good at investing in other people. She works as an academic adviser for a large university. Her dream is to become the president of a private school. She has helped hundreds of students navigate the college-course-selection process and develop a plan to graduate on time. Although Sarah was good at helping others, she allowed negative self-talk to hinder her from realizing her full potential. Sarah would allow her emotions to control her mood. If she felt good about herself one day, she would be happy. If she felt bad about herself the next day, she would go around feeling depressed. Sarah knew that she could eventually become president, but something just didn't add up in her mind. Sarah had had enough of the yo-yo emotions that kept her in a dark place. She started writing positive affirmations and strategically placing them everywhere and anywhere she would see them. She even had an alarm on her phone to remind her to read her daily affirmations. She also started investing in her personal and professional development. She started reading two nonfiction books a month, attending seminars and work-shops, and listening to personal-development pod-casts. What was Sarah doing? She was feeding the champion within. It didn't happen overnight, but eventually she was able to build the mentality of living like a champion. Since then, Sarah has gotten several promotions, and she is well on her way to reaching her career goals.

So stop and ask yourself if you're falling vic-tim to negative thoughts like Sarah was. How do you combat those thoughts? What are you doing to build yourself up daily? Answering these ques-tions will give you a road map to start going in the right direction. There's a war taking place in our hearts and minds. We live in a broken world with real problems, pains, and worries. From radio to television, we are constantly bombarded with negative information. Over time, this negativity can take root and infect other areas of our lives.

Many people become fearful and stressed about the future because of their current situations. I believe we need to start combating every thought or action that does not move us forward.

I heard a story about a Japanese general. During an important battle, the Japanese general decided to attack even though his army was greatly outnumbered. He was confident they would win, but his men were filled with doubt. On the way to battle, they stopped at a spiritual shrine. After praying with the men, the general took out a coin and said, "I shall now toss this coin. If it is heads, we shall win. If tails, we shall lose. Destiny will now reveal itself."

He threw the coin into the air, and all watched intently as it landed. It was heads! The soldiers were so overjoyed and filled with confidence that they vigorously attacked the enemy and were victorious. After the battle, a lieutenant remarked to the general, "No one can change destiny."

"Quite right," the general replied as he showed the lieutenant the coin, which had heads on both sides. The odds may be stacked against you, but the most important thing is to believe that you can succeed! Destiny is revealing itself now. It's heads on both sides of your coin. Friends, incredible power is released when we believe we can do anything we set our minds to. I'm asking you to get rid of the negative thoughts that say things like "I'm always going to be broke," "I will never find the right person," or "I'm not qualified to be in management."

No one can stop you from reaching your fullest potential except you. It starts by declaring that you are a champion and living like one.

In life we're all going to have things come up that will try to keep us from carrying out our purpose in life. But remember, what you have inside you will be brought out when you have the opportunity to be challenged. Start looking at your setbacks as opportunities to blossom like a butterfly. Don't start talking defeatism and complaining. Do what Gerry Arrowood did; discover your inner champion.

If you feel limited by debt, quit complaining about it and start doing something about it.

If you want to get more fulfillment in your career, start focusing on your passion and destiny.

Are you facing a health issue? Start declaring your future is bright, and make plans to live a healthy, whole life.

When was the last time you sat down and thought about the legacy you're passing on to your family? You can build a legacy of freedom.

Remember, if you don't like where you are today, you hold the keys to change it. There's a champion inside you. See the sun now bursting through the clouds. It's your moment to shine. Step up and live like the champion you are destined to be.

Appendix
Financial Management Forms

Go to www.debtfreebie.com to download worksheets

SMART Financial Goal Worksheet 1

Today's Date: _____   Start Date: _____   Target Date: _____

Date Achieved: _____

Financial Goal: _____

Verify that your financial goal is SMART

Specific: *What exactly will you accomplish?*

_____
_____
_____

Measurable: *How will you know when you have reached this goal?*

_____
_____

Achievable: *Have you honestly consider whether you can reach this goal? Have you got the resources to achieve this goal? If not, how will you get them?*

_____
_____
_____

Realistic: *Is achieving this goal realistic with effort and commitment? Why is this goal important to your life?*

_____
_____
_____

Time-bound: *When will you achieve this goal?*

_____
_____
_____

Go to www.debtfreebie.com to download worksheets

This goal is important because:

_____
_____

The benefits of achieving this goal will be:

_____
_____
_____

Take Action!

Potential Obstacles	Potential Solutions
_____	_____
_____	_____
_____	_____
_____	_____
_____	_____
_____	_____
_____	_____

Who are the people I will ask to help me?

_____
_____
_____

Specific Action Steps: *What steps need to be taken to get you to your financial goal?*

What?	Expected Completion Date	Completed
_____	_____	_____
_____	_____	_____
_____	_____	_____
_____	_____	_____
_____	_____	_____

Go to www.debtfreebie.com to download worksheets

⊹ SAMPLE BUDGET WORKSHEET 1			
	Month:		
INCOME		**Budget**	**Actual**
	Salary 1		
	Salary 2		
	Other		
	Other		
	Total Budgeted Income: ➡		**Total Actual Income**
EXPENSES			
Set	Giving		
	Saving		
	Retirement		
	Home Mortgage/Rent		
	Cell/Home Phone		
	Electricity		
	Gas-home		
	Internet		
	Security System		
	Cable		
	Trash		
	Water		
	Car Insurance		
	Health Insurance		
	Home/Renters Insurance		
	Life Insurance		
	Identity Theft Protection		
	Other		
	Other		
	Other		
Debts	Credit Card Payment 1		
	Credit Card Payment 2		
	Other non-mortgage debt		
	Other		
	Total Budgeted Set Expenses: ➡		**Total Actual Set Expenses**

Go to www.debtfreebie.com to download worksheets

SAMPLE BUDGET WORKSHEET 1

Adjustable				
	Books/Magazines	_____		_____
	Child Related Expenses	_____		_____
	*Clothing	_____		_____
	Electronics	_____		_____
	*Entertainment	_____		_____
	*Food	_____		_____
	*Gas/oil change	_____		_____
	Gifts/birthdays	_____		_____
	Gym Membership	_____		_____
	Home Décor	_____		_____
	*Pocket Money	_____		_____
	Job Expense/Parking	_____		_____
	*Personal Care/Toiletries	_____		_____
	Pet Supplies	_____		_____
	Recreation	_____		_____
	Vacation	_____		_____
	Vehicle Maintenance	_____		_____
	Other	_____		_____
	Other	_____		_____
	Other	_____		_____
	Total Budgeted Adjustable Expenses:	➡ _____		**Total Actual Adj. Expenses** _____

Final Totals	Total Budgeted Income	_____		Actual Monthly Income	_____
	minus	-		minus	-
	Total Budgeted Expenses	_____		Actual Monthly Expenses	_____
	Total Budgeted Balance	_____		Actual Monthly Balance	_____

Go to www.debtfreebie.com to download worksheets

SAMPLE BUDGET WORKSHEET 1

The above "Total
Budgeted Balance"
number should
equal zero

*See note on
"Actual Monthly
Balance" below

Notes:

1. Use the "Actual" column to keep track of what you really earn and spend throughout the month.

2. Keep in mind, in a zero-based budget the "Total Budgeted Balance" must always equal zero.

3. If the "Actual Monthly Balance" doesn't equal zero at the end of the month because you spent less than you budgeted, then that's great! Move the extra money into another category - preferably places like savings, retirement, or paying extra on debt or towards the mortgage.

4. Categories with a * can be used for envelop system.

5. If you need any assistance or have a question, email coach.ivory@debtfreebie.com

The Debt Snowball
Worksheet 3

The Debt Snowball method will dramatically accelerate paying of your debt. The main purpose of the Debt Snowball is to build on your payments, after you have paid a smaller debt. Paying the little debts off first gives you quick wins, and you are more likely to stay with the plan. Now is the time to knock out that debt!

Step 1. List all your debts in order, from the smallest balance to the largest. (Don't worry about interest rates, unless two debts have a similar pay off balance. In that case, list the one with the higher balance first.

Step 2. Go crazy on that smallest debt as much as you possibly can. Every extra dollar you can get your hands on should be thrown at that smallest debt until it is gone. Once you pay one debt off, take what you were paying on that one and add it to the minimum payment of the next debt. As the snowball rolls over, it gets bigger and bigger... get it?

Step 3. Every time you pay off a debt, cross the debt off. This will show you how close you're getting to becoming debt-free!

NOTE: The "New Payment" is the total of the previous debt's payment PLUS the current debt's minimum.

Debts	Total Payoff	Minimum Payment	New Payment

Your Best Life = Action!